1·2·3 Draw
CARTOON ANIMALS

A step-by-step guide

by Steve Barr

PEEL PRODUCTIONS, INC.

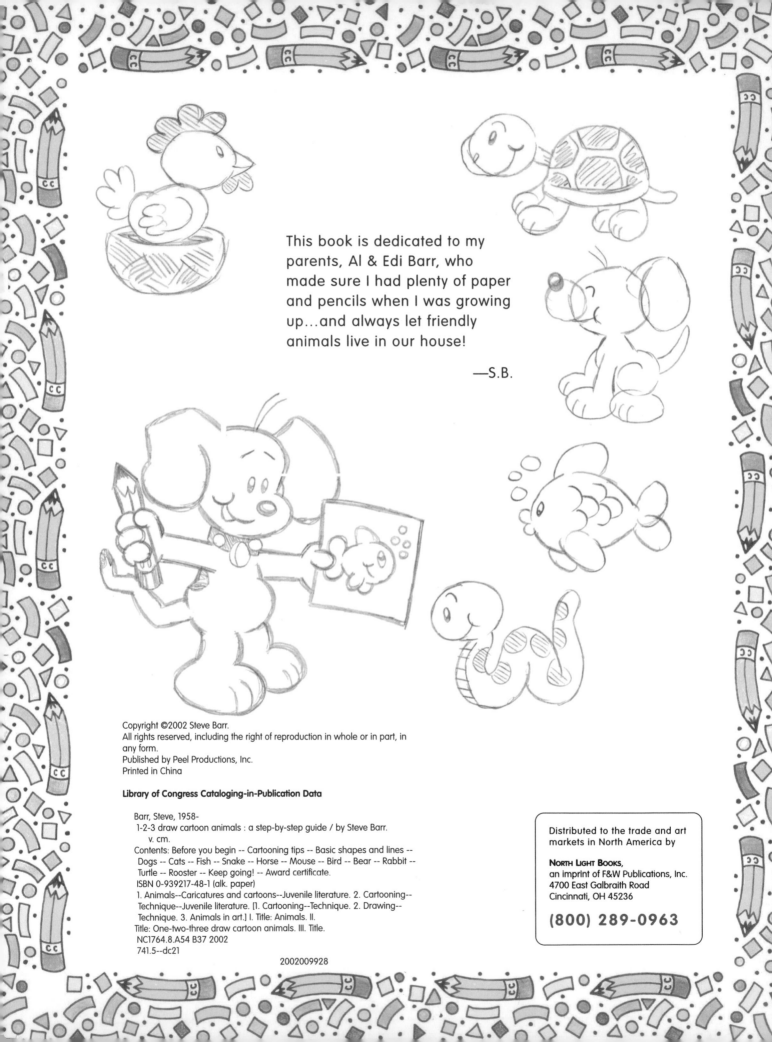

This book is dedicated to my parents, Al & Edi Barr, who made sure I had plenty of paper and pencils when I was growing up…and always let friendly animals live in our house!

—S.B.

Published by Peel Productions, Inc.
Printed in China

Library of Congress Cataloging-in-Publication Data

Barr, Steve, 1958-
  1-2-3 draw cartoon animals : a step-by-step guide / by Steve Barr.
    v. cm.
  Contents: Before you begin -- Cartooning tips -- Basic shapes and lines -- Dogs -- Cats -- Fish -- Snake -- Horse -- Mouse -- Bird -- Bear -- Rabbit -- Turtle -- Rooster -- Keep going! -- Award certificate.
  ISBN 0-939217-48-1 (alk. paper)
  1. Animals--Caricatures and cartoons--Juvenile literature. 2. Cartooning--Technique--Juvenile literature. [1. Cartooning--Technique. 2. Drawing--Technique. 3. Animals in art.] I. Title: Animals. II.
Title: One-two-three draw cartoon animals. III. Title.
NC1764.8.A54 B37 2002
741.5--dc21
                                  2002009928

Distributed to the trade and art markets in North America by

NORTH LIGHT BOOKS,
an imprint of F&W Publications, Inc.
4700 East Galbraith Road
Cincinnati, OH 45236

(800) 289-0963

Contents

Before you begin,

you will need the following supplies:

- A pencil (or pencils!)
- An eraser
- A pencil sharpener
- LOTS of paper
- Colored pencils, markers or crayons
- A good light source
- A comfortable place to draw
- Your imagination!

Now, let's begin!

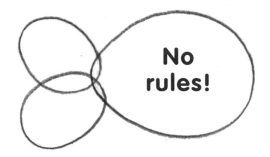

No rules!

Use this book as a basic guide to drawing cartoon animals with simple shapes. If I draw an oval and you feel like drawing a triangle, draw a triangle. If your drawing looks funny… congratulations! You have created a cartoon! That's what cartoons are, funny pictures.

Cartooning tips:

1 Draw lightly at first—SKETCH, so you can erase extra lines.

2 Practice, practice, practice! You will get better and your cartoons will get funnier!

3 Have FUN cartooning!

The best part of cartooning is… There are NO RULES! Look at the comics in a newspaper or cartoons on TV. They all look different from each other, because all cartoonists have their own style of drawing.

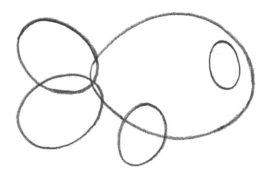

Sketch, doodle, play!

Experiment! Make your very own creation. Change anything you want. Color your cartoon any color you wish. Create your own cartoon style.

Basic Shapes and Lines

Here are the basic shapes and lines you will use to draw cartoons:

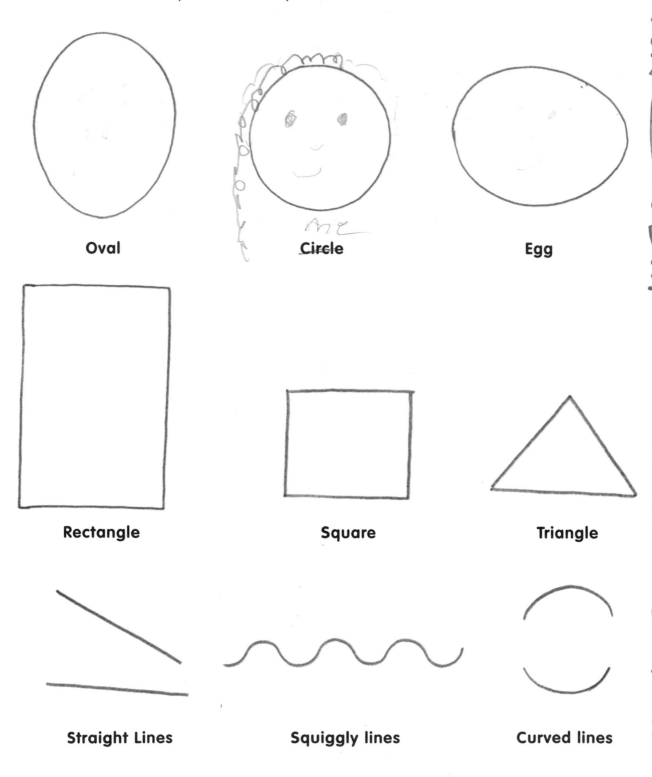

Oval

Circle

Egg

Rectangle

Square

Triangle

Straight Lines

Squiggly lines

Curved lines

Dogs

Everyone loves a fun dog, so let's begin by drawing cartoon dogs. LOOK at the faces of these two happy hounds! See the shapes and lines used to create their unique expressions.

Dog's Face

Let's start with a side view of a cartoon dog's face. We will draw the body later.

1 Lightly sketch an **oval** and an **egg** for the dog's ear and head. Notice that they overlap.

2 Draw two small **ovals** for the eye.

3 Darken part of the eye. Sketch a **curved line** to begin the nose.

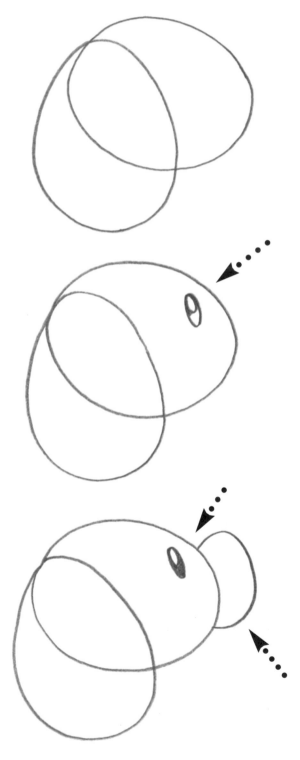

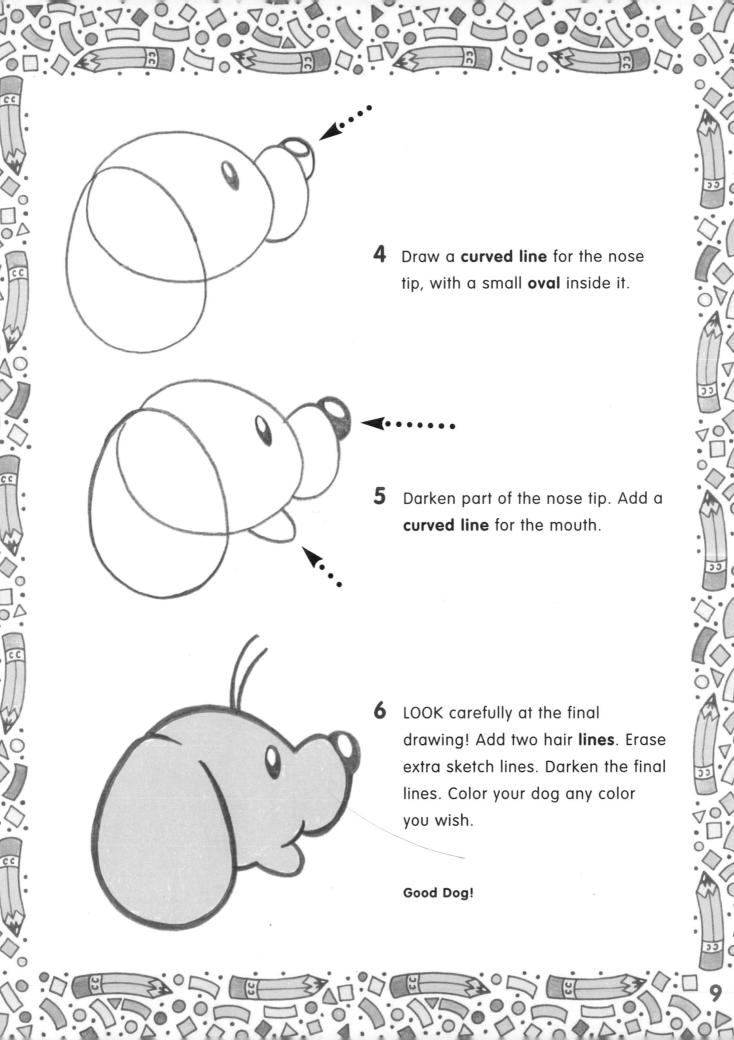

4 Draw a **curved line** for the nose tip, with a small **oval** inside it.

5 Darken part of the nose tip. Add a **curved line** for the mouth.

6 LOOK carefully at the final drawing! Add two hair **lines**. Erase extra sketch lines. Darken the final lines. Color your dog any color you wish.

Good Dog!

Now, let's draw a front view of a dog's face.

1   Sketch two overlapping **ovals**.

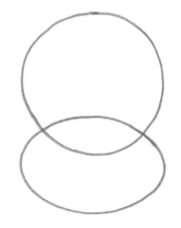

2   Sketch two **ovals** for each eye. Sketch another **oval** for the nose.

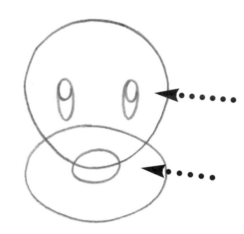

3   Sketch **curved lines** to begin the ears. Darken part of the eyes and nose.

4 Sketch two more **ovals** for the ends of the ears.

5 Draw a **curved line** and a **straight line** to make the tongue.

6 LOOK at the final drawing! Erase extra sketch lines. Darken the final lines. Add color.

Bow-WOW! You are talented!

Let's draw a body for the dog. When you draw his head, make sure you leave plenty of room on the paper for his body.

1 Draw the side view of the dog's face again. (See page 8 for details.)

2 Sketch an **oval** for the body.

3 Draw six **straight lines** for the legs.

4 Sketch **ovals** and **curved lines** for the feet.

5 Draw a tail.

6 LOOK at the final drawing! Erase extra sketch lines. Darken final lines. Add curved lines to his feet for paws. Add a couple of **curved lines** near his tail to make it look like it's wagging! Add color.

Happy Dog!

You can make cartoon animals look and act human if you draw them standing up, talking, or wearing clothes! Let's try doing that with the front-view dog face you drew before.

1 Draw the front view of the dog's face again. (See page 10 for details.) Leave plenty of room for the body!

Draw a short **line** under his head for the neck.

Sketch a large **oval** for the body.

Draw three **straight lines** for legs.

Sketch two overlapping **ovals** for his feet.

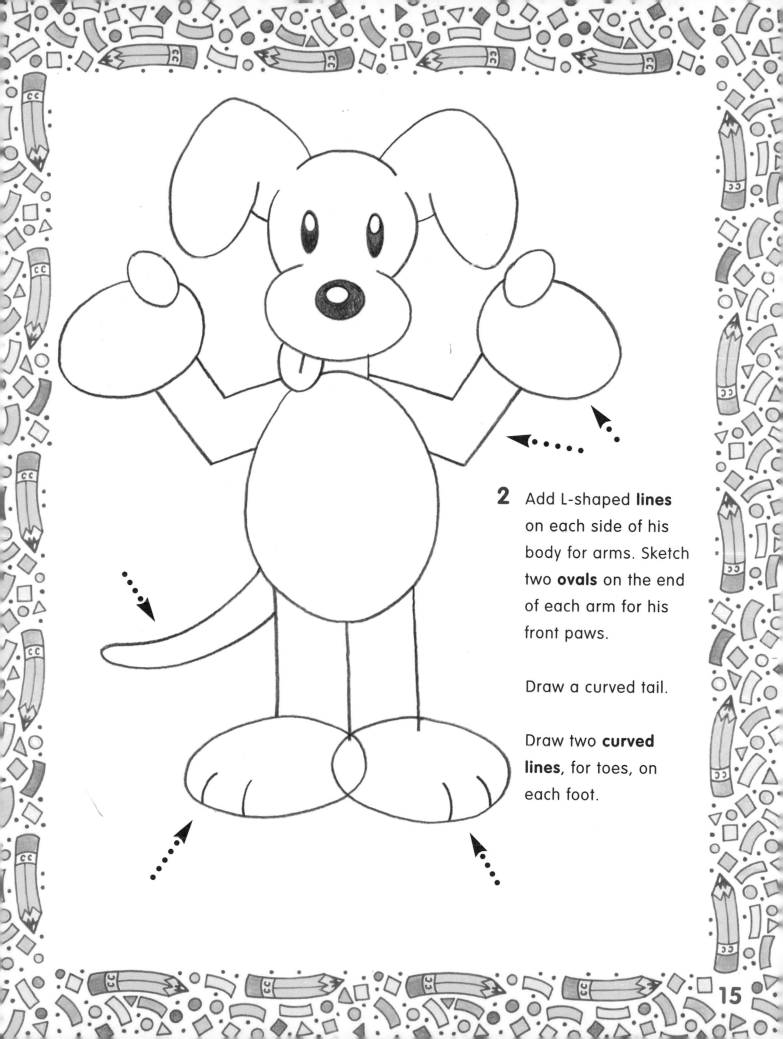

2 Add L-shaped **lines** on each side of his body for arms. Sketch two **ovals** on the end of each arm for his front paws.

Draw a curved tail.

Draw two **curved lines**, for toes, on each foot.

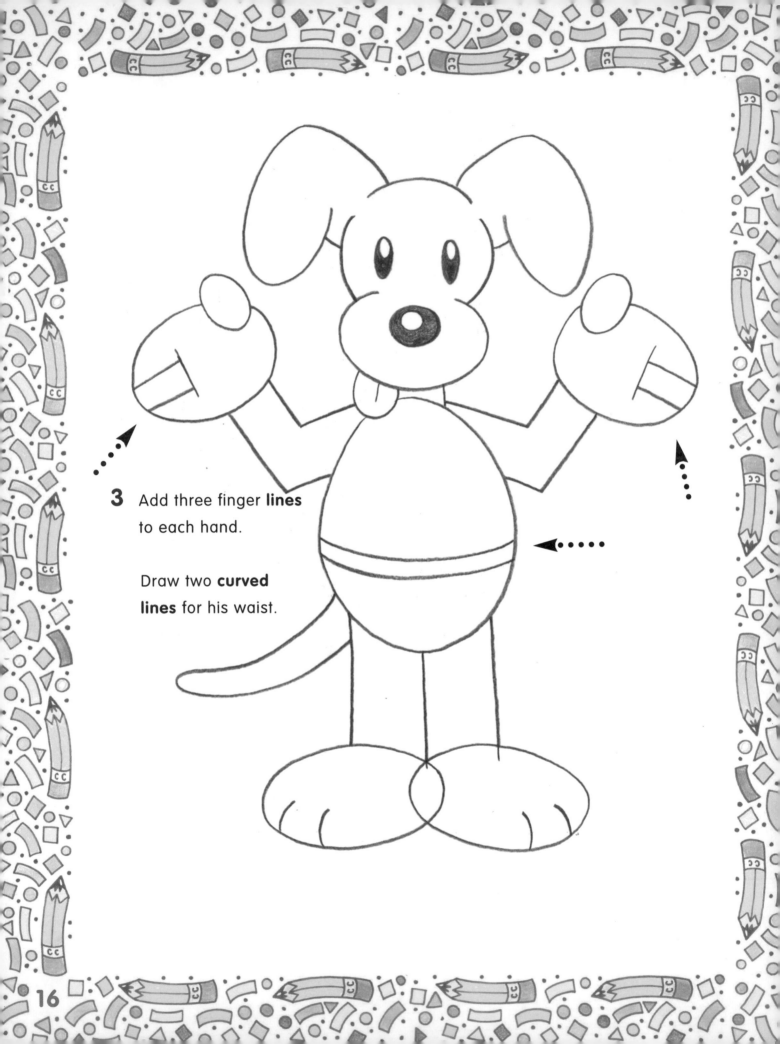

3 Add three finger **lines**
to each hand.

Draw two **curved**
lines for his waist.

4 LOOK at the final drawing! Erase extra sketch lines. Darken the final lines and add color.

Artist's Tip:

Cartoon animals can be as human as you want to make them! Try drawing this dog again. Give him a name! Give him more clothes and a wild hat.

Puppy

1 Lightly sketch three overlapping **ovals** for the ear, head and body.

2 Starting at the top, sketch an **oval** for the eye. Draw **curved lines** for the tail. Sketch two **ovals** for feet.

3 Add two **curved lines** to the eye. Draw **curved lines** to form the nose, the chin, and the other two legs.

4 Darken part of the nose and eye. Add **curved lines** to his paws.

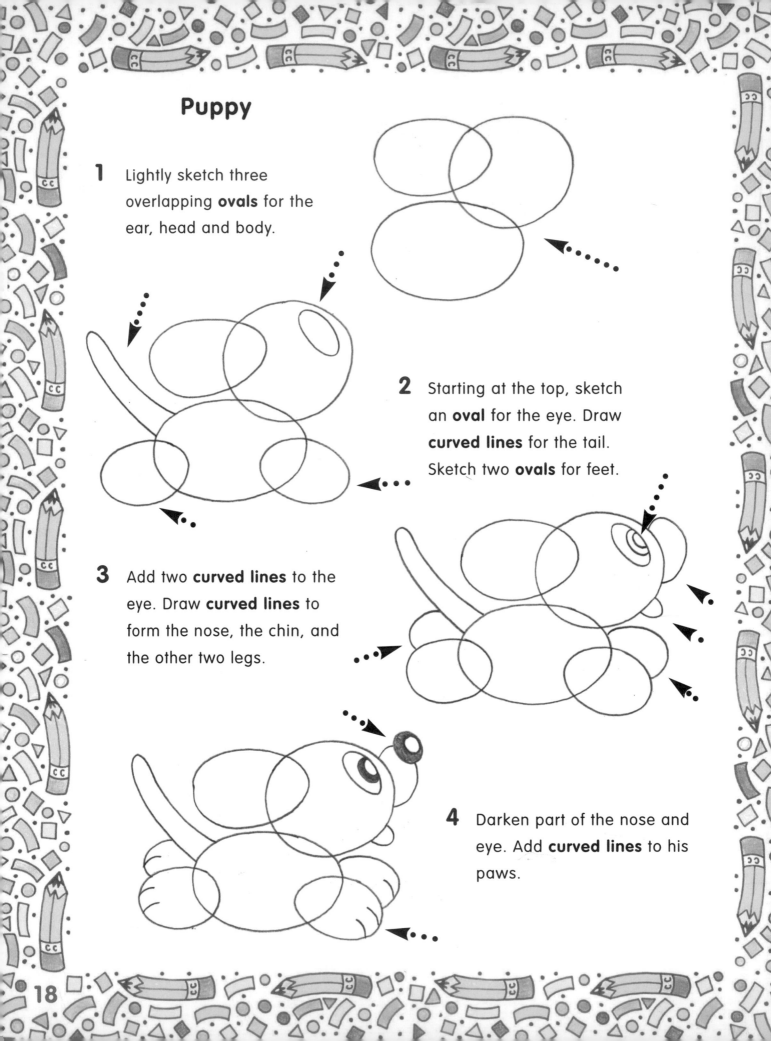

5 Add four "wagging" **lines** near his tail, and you have a happy puppy lying down. Or... draw some grass underneath him, add "running" **lines**. Wow! He's off and running!

6 LOOK at the final drawing! Erase extra sketch lines. Darken the final lines and add color.

Cats

Let's start with a front view of a cat face. We'll draw the body later.

1 Sketch a wide **oval** with slightly pointed ends for the cat's face.

2 Sketch **triangle** ears. Draw a small **triangle** for the nose.

3 Draw two **ovals** with **circles** inside them for eyes. Add an **oval** inside the nose. Draw a **curved line** with small **curved lines** on each side to make a big grinning mouth.

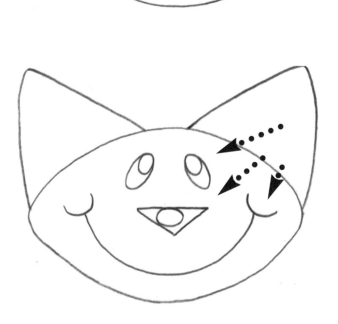

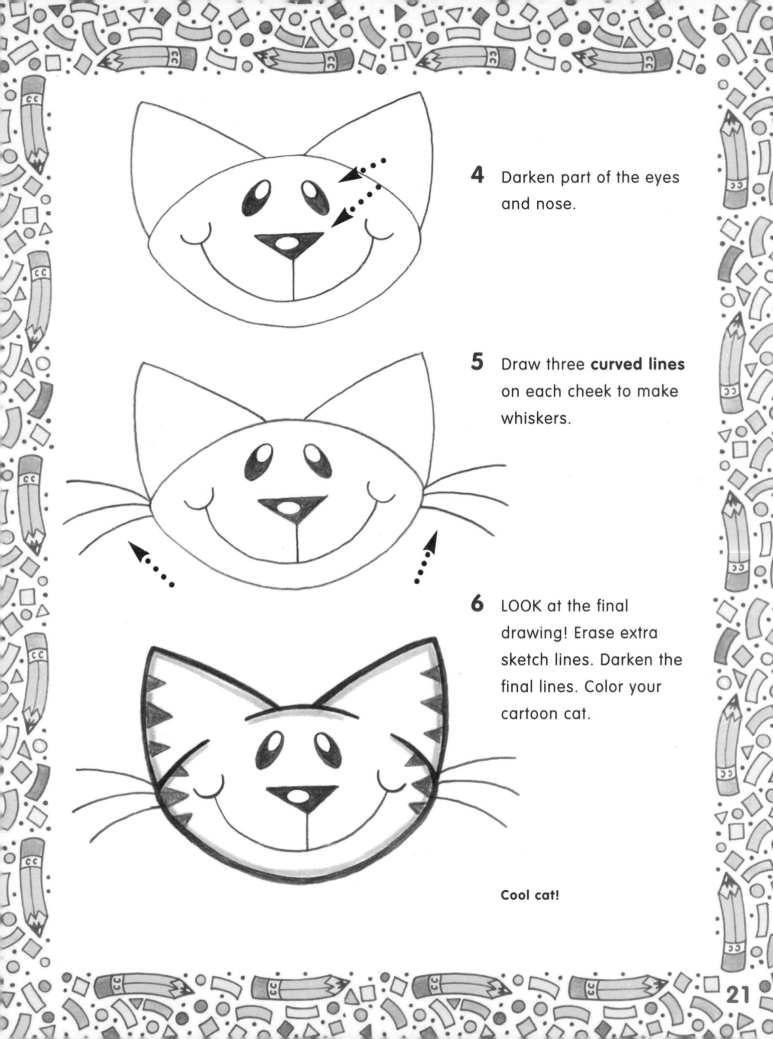

4 Darken part of the eyes and nose.

5 Draw three **curved lines** on each cheek to make whiskers.

6 LOOK at the final drawing! Erase extra sketch lines. Darken the final lines. Color your cartoon cat.

Cool cat!

Now, let's draw a side view of a cat's face. We'll add a body later.

1 Sketch a large **oval** for the head and a small **oval** for the eye.

2 Draw two **triangles** to make an ear. Draw another **oval** inside the eye. Add a **curved line** for the jaw.

3 Draw the other ear. Add another **oval** inside the eye. Look at the nose and nose tip. Draw the shapes you see.

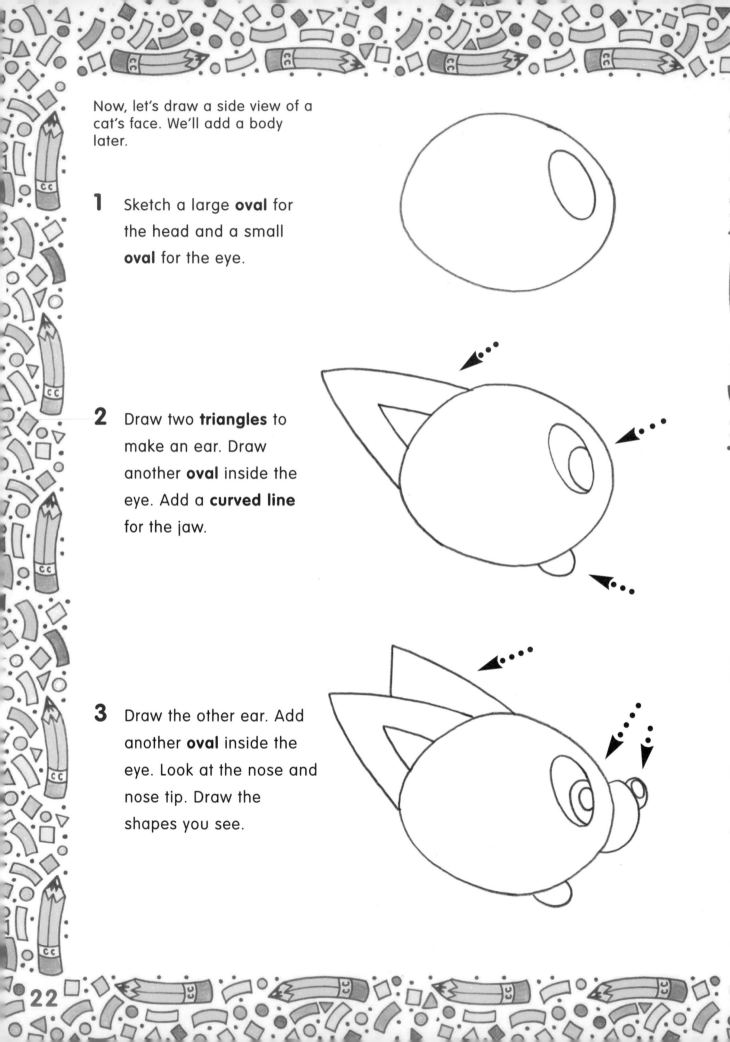

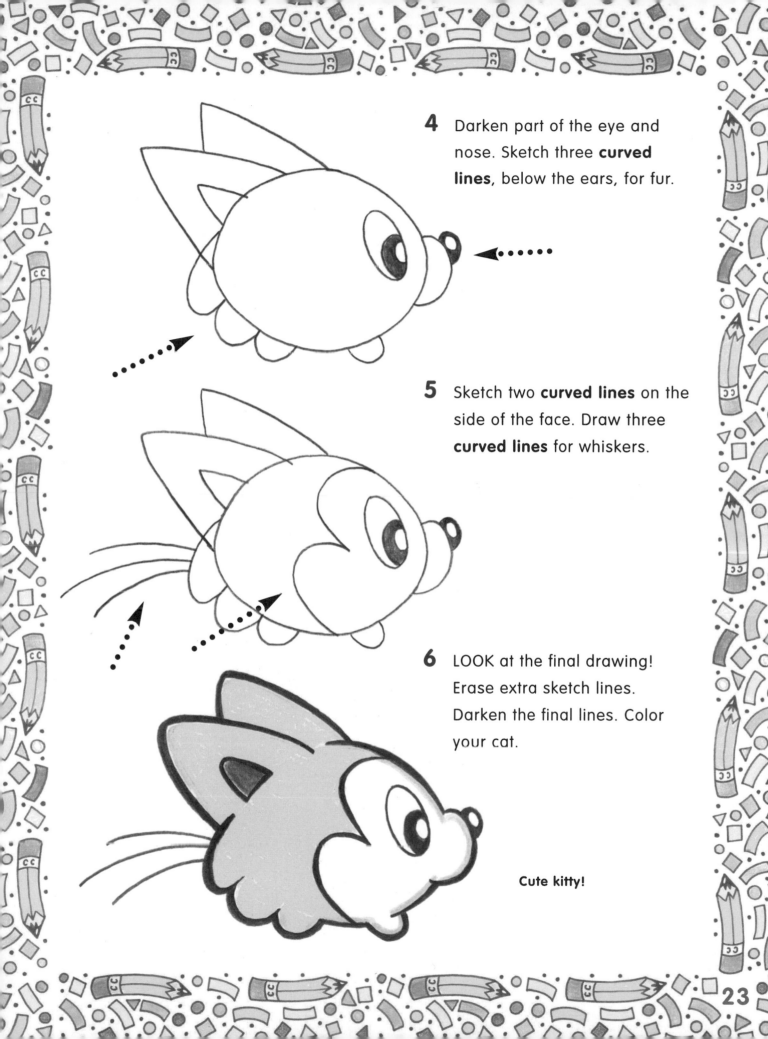

4 Darken part of the eye and nose. Sketch three **curved lines**, below the ears, for fur.

5 Sketch two **curved lines** on the side of the face. Draw three **curved lines** for whiskers.

6 LOOK at the final drawing! Erase extra sketch lines. Darken the final lines. Color your cat.

Cute kitty!

Now let's give that cute little kitten a body.

1 Lightly sketch the side view of her head again. (See page 22 for details.)

2 Sketch an **oval** for the body.

3 Sketch two **ovals** and a **curved line** for legs.

4 Draw **curved lines** to make a big, fluffy tail. Add two **curved lines** to each foot to make paws.

5 LOOK at the final drawing! Erase extra sketch lines. Darken the final lines and color

Purrrr-fect!

Let's make the cartoon cat look human.

1 Sketch the front view of a cat's head again. (See page 20 for details.) Draw it at the top of the paper so you have room to add the body.

Sketch a large **oval** for the body. Draw **straight lines** for the legs. At the bottom of each leg, sketch an **oval** for the foot.

2 Draw a long **looping line** for the arm.

Draw a long, slightly curving tail.

Draw **curved lines** to add paws to each foot.

27

3 Draw a **triangle** under his chin.

Draw two **curved lines** on his hand.

Draw another **curved line** to make his shirt sleeve. Add two **circles** for buttons. Draw a curved waist **line**, with a little **triangle** under the buttons.

4 LOOK at the final drawing! Erase extra sketch lines. Darken the final lines and color.

Good looking cat!

Add some "walking" or "wagging" lines to make him really move!

Fish

Here's a quick way to draw a cute cartoon fish.

1 Lightly sketch three overlapping **ovals** for the body and tail.

2 Sketch an **oval** for a fin, and one for the eye.

dorsal fin

3 Sketch a curved shape for the **dorsal fin**. Darken part of the eye. Draw the mouth. Sketch a **curved line** for the other fin.

4 LOOK at the final drawing! Erase extra sketch lines. Darken final lines. Shade and color. Add bubbles.

Fun and funny fish!

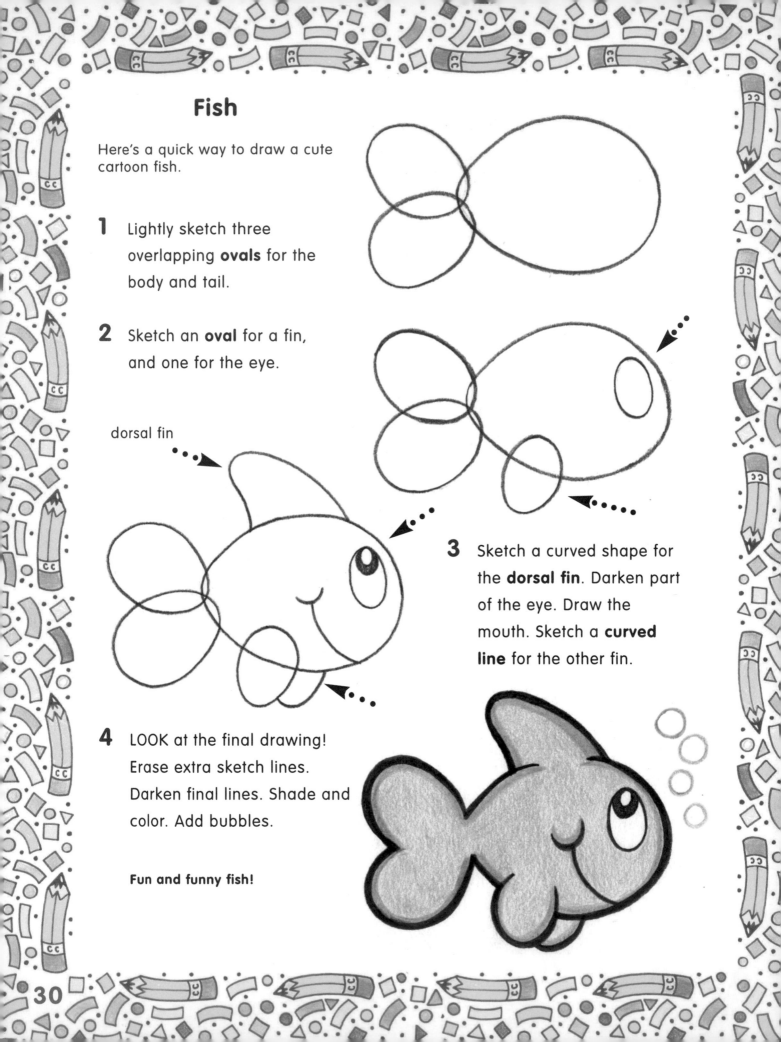

Snake

Let's draw a snake with a surprise ending.

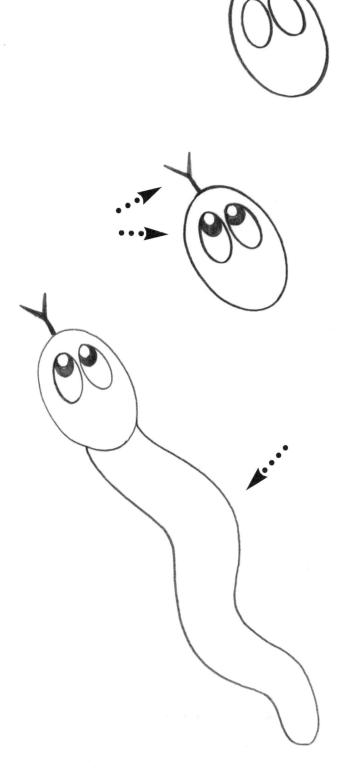

1 Sketch an **oval** for the head. Draw two **ovals** inside it for eyes.

2 Add a "Y" shape for a tongue. Darken part of the eyes.

3 Draw a big **squiggly line** for the snake's body.

4 Add **curved lines** along the body.

You can color it now, and you will have a wonderful cartoon snake.

Or...

5 ...KEEP GOING! Draw 4 pairs of **curved lines** coming out from the snake's body.

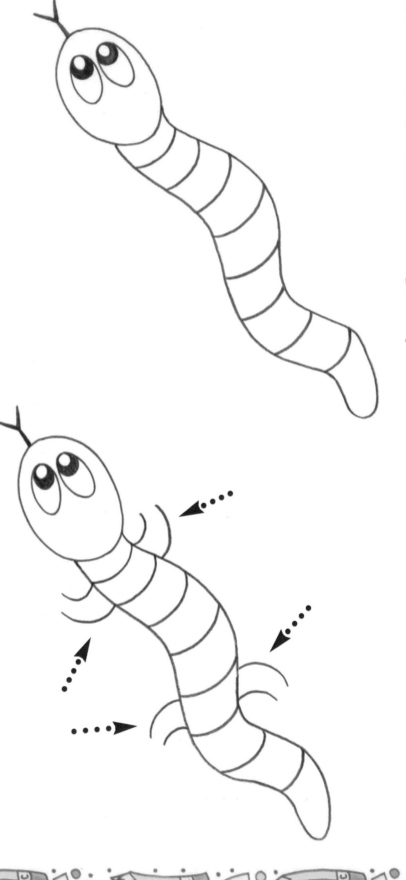

6 Sketch an **oval** at the end of the **curved lines** to make a foot. Sketch four smaller **ovals** on each foot for toes.

7 LOOK at the final drawing! Erase extra sketch lines. Darken the final lines. Color your lizard.

Incredible cartoon lizard!

Hang him on your refrigerator door so everyone can see what a talented cartoonist you are!

33

Horse

Let's draw a cartoon horse's head.

1 Lightly sketch two overlapping **ovals** for the head and the ear.

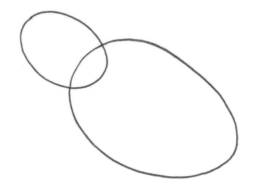

2 Sketch a smaller **oval** inside the ear. Sketch three **ovals** for the eye. Draw a **curved line** across the face. Draw two **straight lines** for the neck.

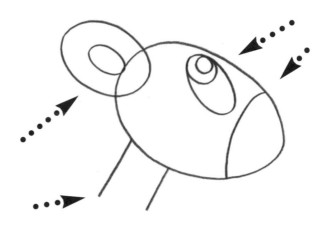

3 Darken part of the eye. Add a small **oval** for the nose.

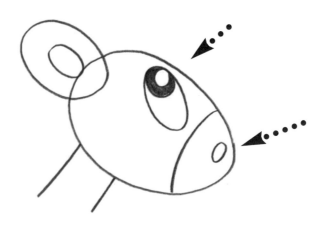

4 Draw big, looping **curved lines** to form the horse's mane.

5 Draw two **curved lines** to make a smiling mouth.

6 LOOK at the final drawing! Erase extra sketch lines. Darken the final lines. Color your cartoon horse's head.

Let's draw the horse, head to tail.
Be sure to leave space at the
bottom of your paper for the
horse's body.

1 Draw the horse's head
again. (See page 34 for
details.)

2 Sketch a large **oval** below
the horse's neck. Add six
straight lines, below it, for
the legs.

3 Sketch a large, fluffy tail with **curved lines**.

hooves

Draw **curved lines**, at the bottom of each leg. Add **lines** for hooves.

4 LOOK at the final drawing!
Add three eyelash **lines**.
Erase extra sketch lines.
Darken the final lines.
Shade and color your
horse!

Happy horse!

Mouse

Let's draw a fun cartoon mouse's head.

1 Sketch three overlapping **ovals** for the mouse's ear, head, and nose.

2 Starting from the left, sketch a smaller **oval**, inside the big **oval**, for the ear hole. Sketch an **oval** for the eye. Draw a **circle** for the nose tip.

3 Draw two more **ovals**, inside the eye, for the eyeball. Add another **oval** inside the nose **oval**.

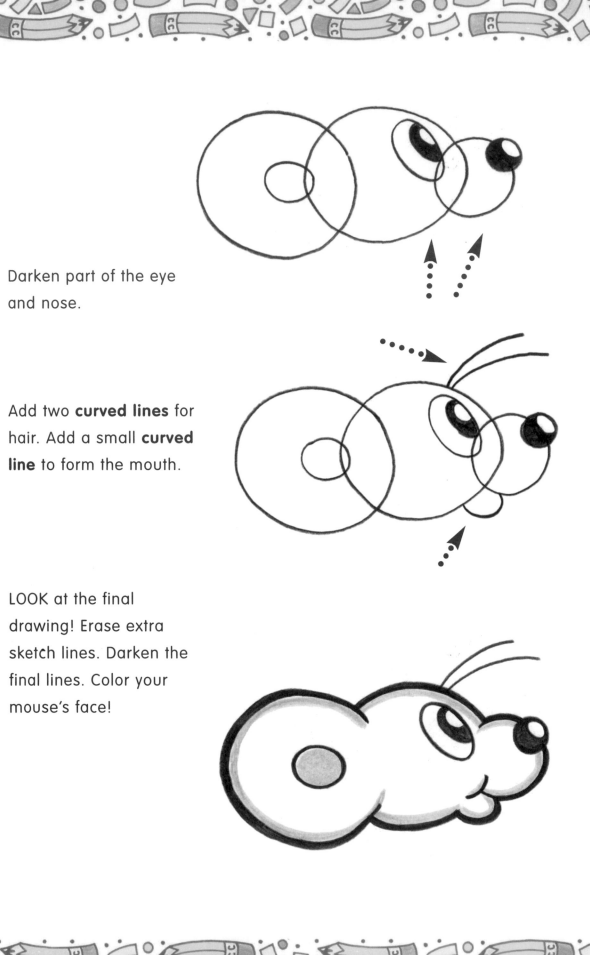

4 Darken part of the eye and nose.

5 Add two **curved lines** for hair. Add a small **curved line** to form the mouth.

6 LOOK at the final drawing! Erase extra sketch lines. Darken the final lines. Color your mouse's face!

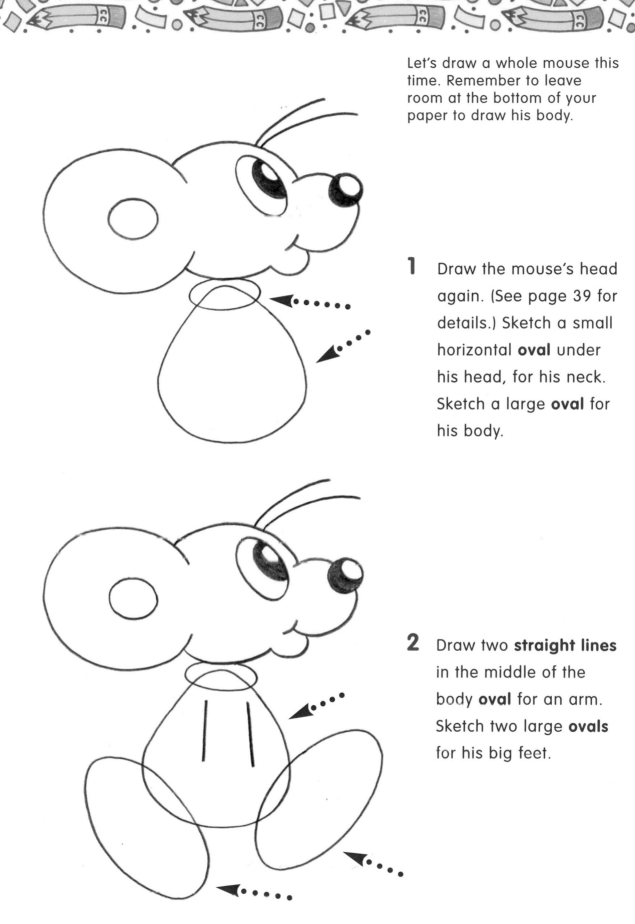

Let's draw a whole mouse this time. Remember to leave room at the bottom of your paper to draw his body.

1 Draw the mouse's head again. (See page 39 for details.) Sketch a small horizontal **oval** under his head, for his neck. Sketch a large **oval** for his body.

2 Draw two **straight lines** in the middle of the body **oval** for an arm. Sketch two large **ovals** for his big feet.

3 Draw a **curved line** at the end of the arm. Draw three small **ovals** for fingers.

4 Draw the **curved** waist **line**. Add two **curved lines** on each foot for paws. Draw a **squiggly line** for his tail.

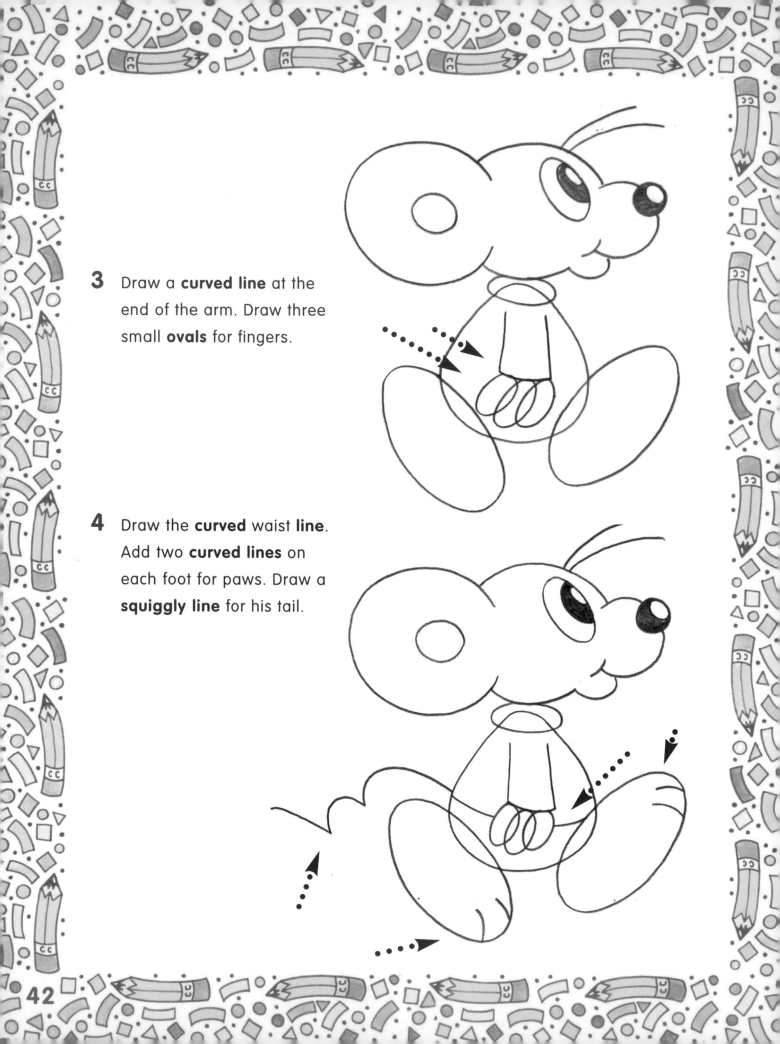

5 Draw another **squiggly line**, under the first one, to complete the tail.

6 LOOK at the final drawing! Erase extra sketch lines. Darken the final lines. Color your cartoon mouse.

Cool mouseneck sweater!

Good job!

Bird

1 Sketch a large **oval** and a smaller, flatter **oval** for the bird's head and eye. Sketch another **oval** for the body.

2 Darken part of the eye. Sketch another **oval**, inside the body **oval**, for the wing. Draw two **straight lines** for the tail. Draw two **straight lines** for the leg. Sketch an **oval** for a foot.

3 Sketch three **ovals** for the tail feathers. Add a small **oval** and two **straight lines** to the foot.

4 Starting at the top, add two curved hair **lines**. Draw two **triangles** for the bird's beak. Draw **lines** for the other leg and foot. Add two **straight lines** for feathers on the wing.

5 LOOK at the final drawing! Erase extra sketch lines. Darken the final lines. Color your cartoon bird.

Beautiful bird!

Bet you could teach your friends and family how to draw!

Bear

1 Sketch two overlapping **ovals** for the bear's body and head.

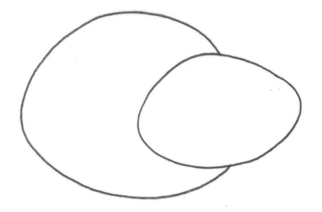

2 Sketch two **curved lines** for the ears. Draw five short **lines** for the legs.

3 Sketch smaller **curved lines** inside the ears. Sketch three **ovals** for the feet. Sketch three small **circles** for the tail.

4 Draw **ovals** for the eyes and nose. Add **lines** for the paws.

5 Darken part of the eyes and nose. Add **curved lines** for the mouth.

6 LOOK at the final drawing! Erase extra sketch lines. Color your cartoon bear.

Beaming bear!

Now let's try drawing a cartoon bear in a sitting position.

1 Sketch two large overlapping **ovals** for the head and body. Sketch two smaller **ovals** for ears.

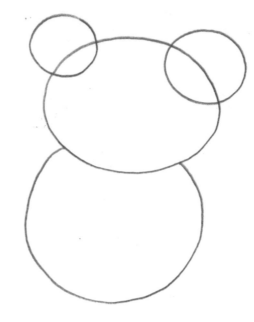

2 Sketch a small **circle** inside each ear. Draw small **ovals** for eyes and nose. Sketch large **ovals** for the feet.

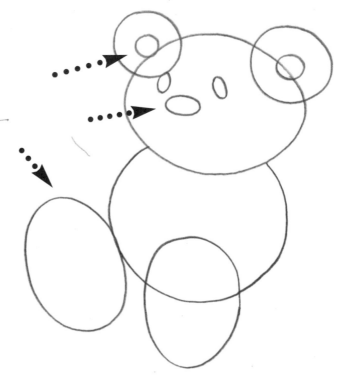

me

cute

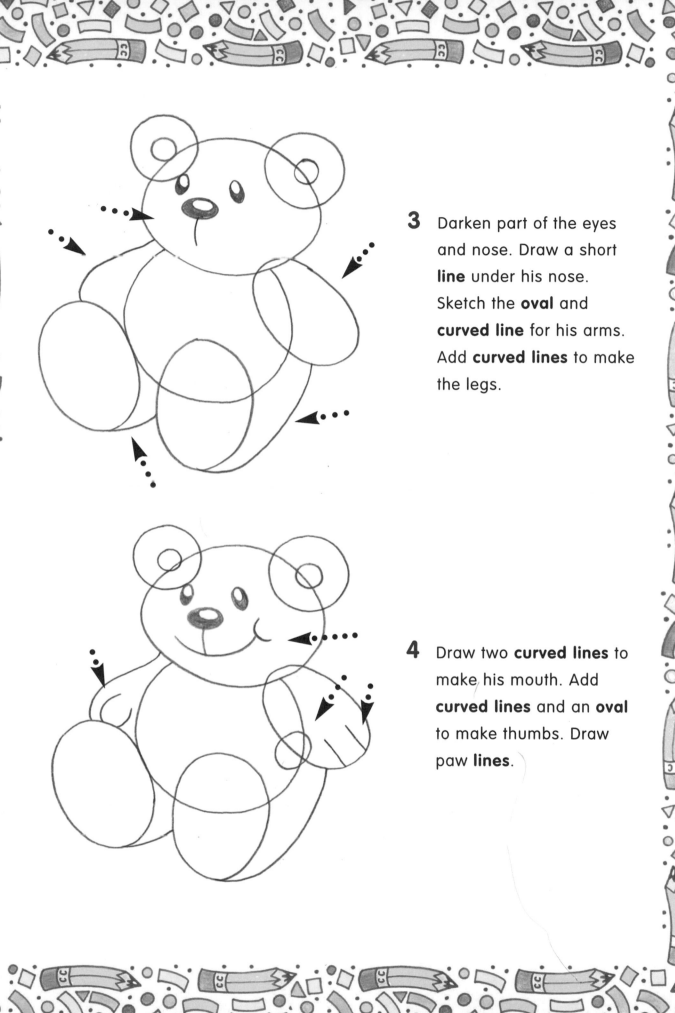

3 Darken part of the eyes and nose. Draw a short **line** under his nose. Sketch the **oval** and **curved line** for his arms. Add **curved lines** to make the legs.

4 Draw two **curved lines** to make his mouth. Add **curved lines** and an **oval** to make thumbs. Draw paw **lines**.

5 Erase extra sketch lines and you would have a beautiful drawing of a sitting bear. But let's add some fur and make him extra fluffy...

6 LOOK at the final drawing! Draw **squiggly lines** for fur all around the outside of the bear. Color your bear.

Nice job! He looks great!

Rabbit

Let's draw a cartoon rabbit.

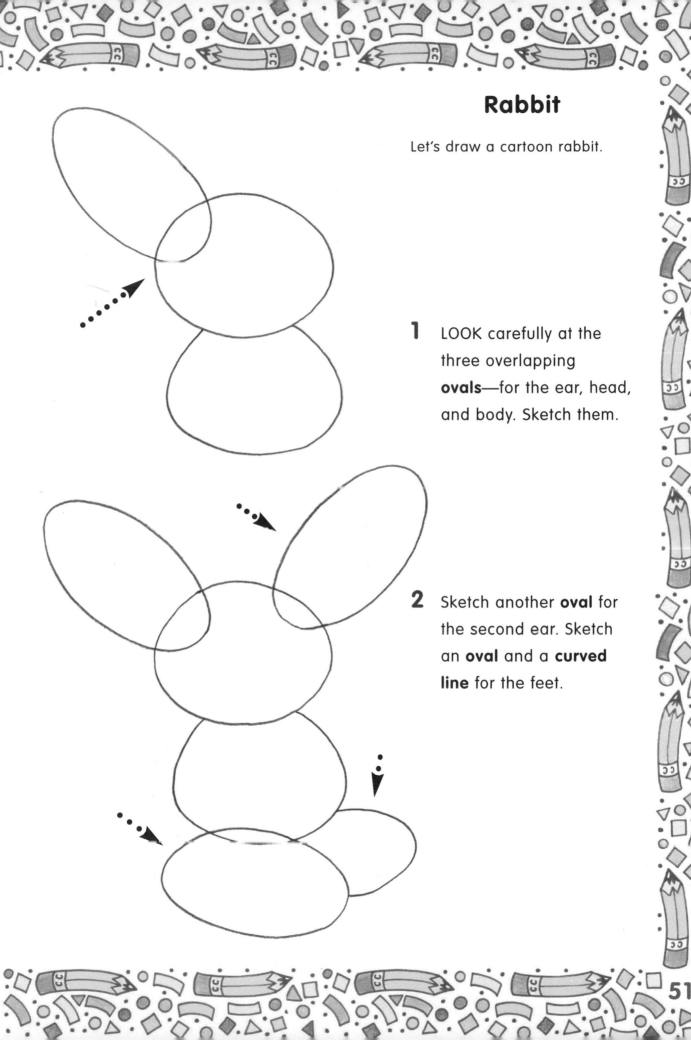

1 LOOK carefully at the three overlapping **ovals**—for the ear, head, and body. Sketch them.

2 Sketch another **oval** for the second ear. Sketch an **oval** and a **curved line** for the feet.

3 Sketch an **oval** inside each of the ears. Sketch two small **ovals** for eyes. Sketch an **oval** for one arm, and a **curved line** for the other arm.

4 Draw a small **circle** inside each eye. Draw a **triangle** for the nose. Sketch **ovals** for thumbs. Add **curved lines** for the paws.

5 Darken part of the eyes and nose. Add **curved lines** to make a smiling mouth. Draw **straight lines** for fingers. Add a **curved line** for the tail.

6 LOOK at the final drawing! Erase extra sketch lines. Add three curved lines on each cheek for whiskers. Color your cartoon rabbit.

Try drawing him again. Give him some fun clothes!

Turtle

A cartoon turtle is really fun to draw. Let's give it a try!

1 Sketch two overlapping **ovals** for the head and eye. Draw two slightly **curved lines** for the neck

2 Sketch a small **oval** at the base of the neck. Draw a large arching **curved line** on top and a slightly **curved line** beneath it for the shell.

3 Darken part of the eye. Draw two **curved lines** to make the mouth. Draw a **curved line** for the bottom of his body.

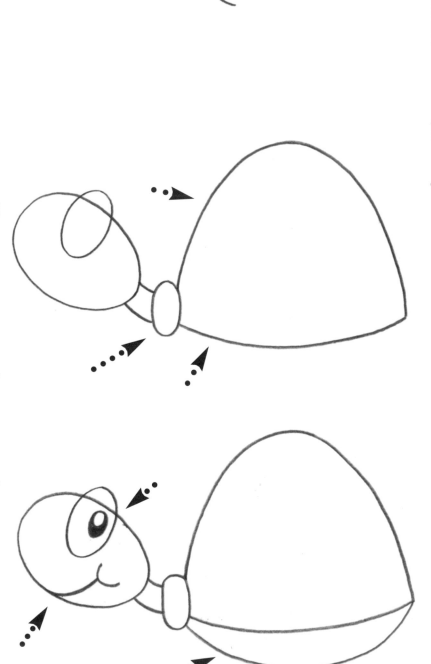

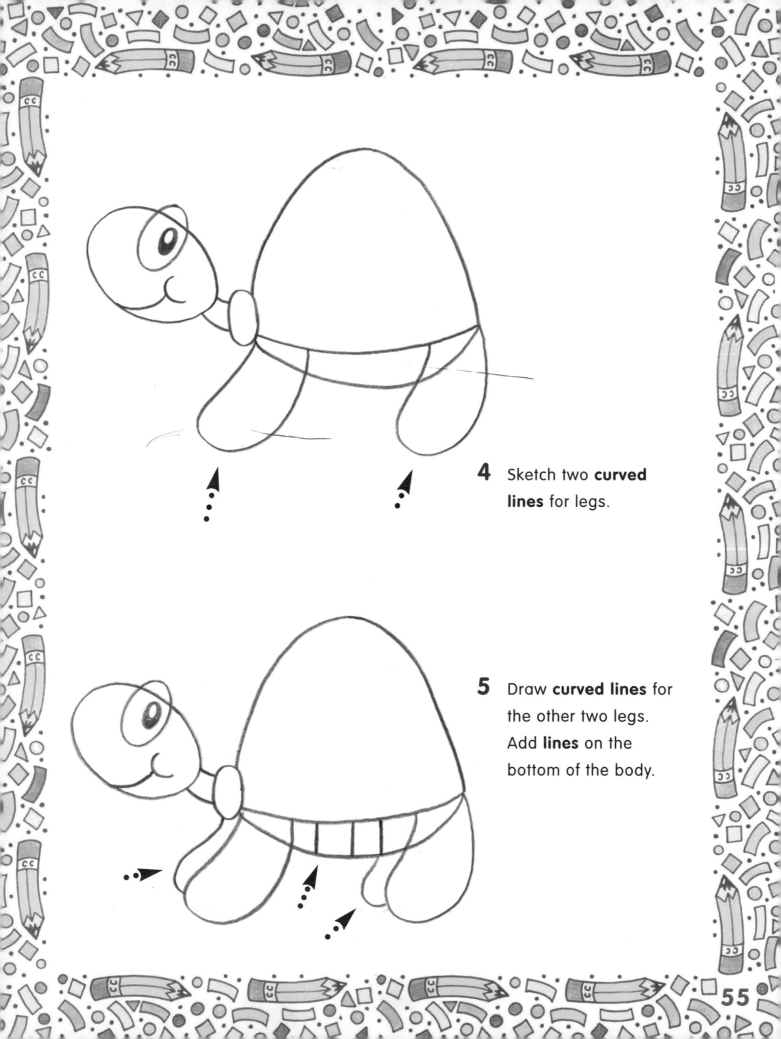

4 Sketch two **curved lines** for legs.

5 Draw **curved lines** for the other two legs. Add **lines** on the bottom of the body.

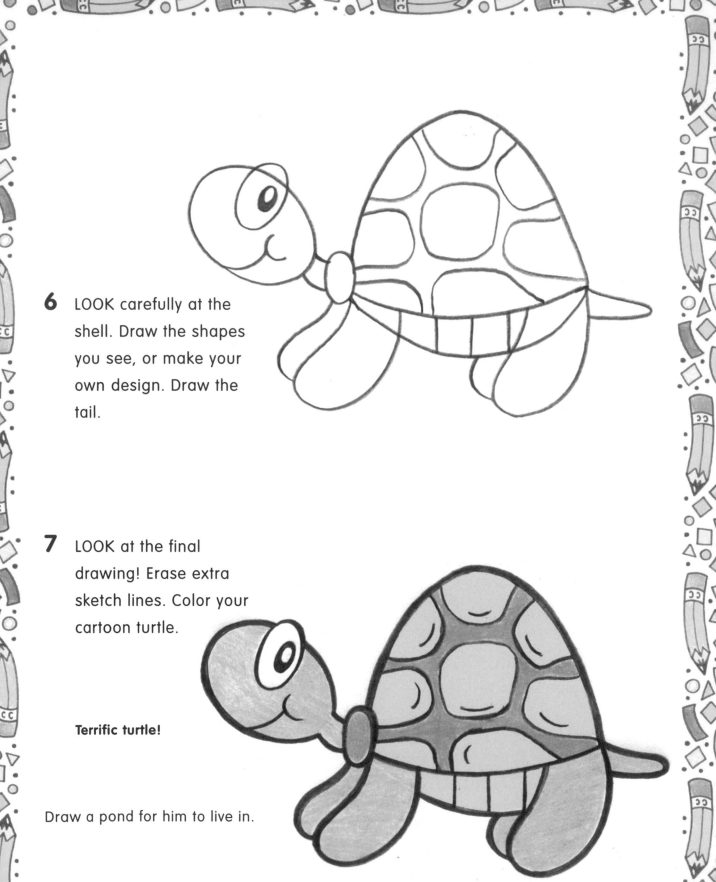

6 LOOK carefully at the shell. Draw the shapes you see, or make your own design. Draw the tail.

7 LOOK at the final drawing! Erase extra sketch lines. Color your cartoon turtle.

Terrific turtle!

Draw a pond for him to live in.

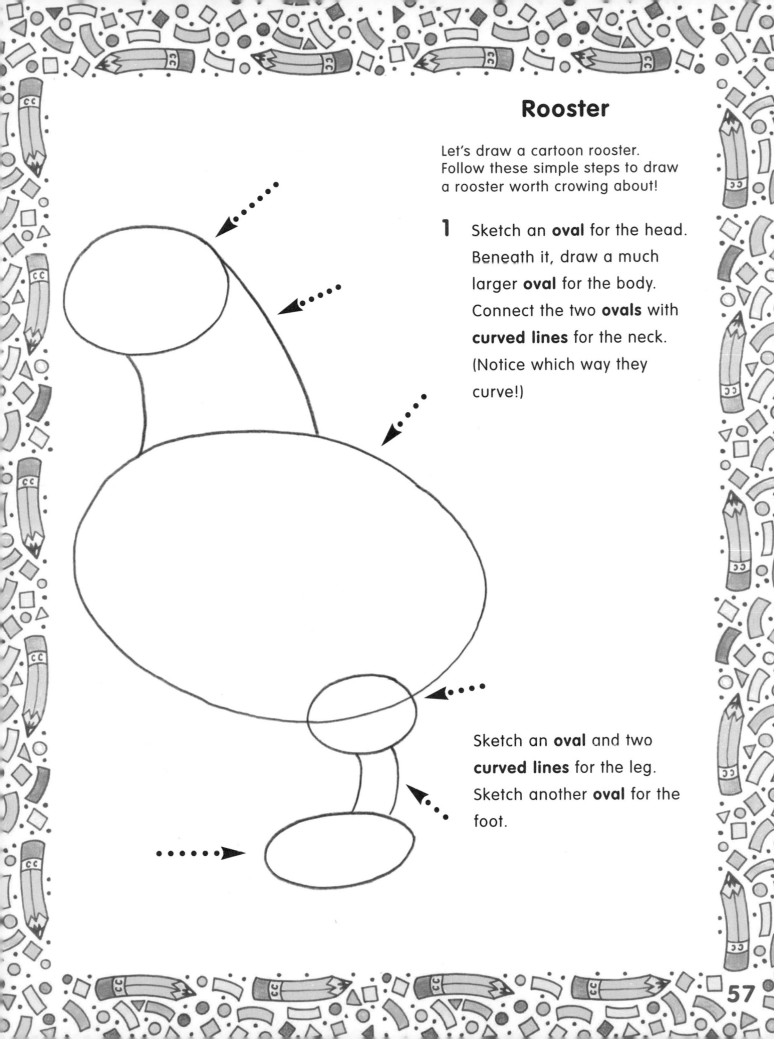

Rooster

Let's draw a cartoon rooster. Follow these simple steps to draw a rooster worth crowing about!

1 Sketch an **oval** for the head. Beneath it, draw a much larger **oval** for the body. Connect the two **ovals** with **curved lines** for the neck. (Notice which way they curve!)

Sketch an **oval** and two **curved lines** for the leg. Sketch another **oval** for the foot.

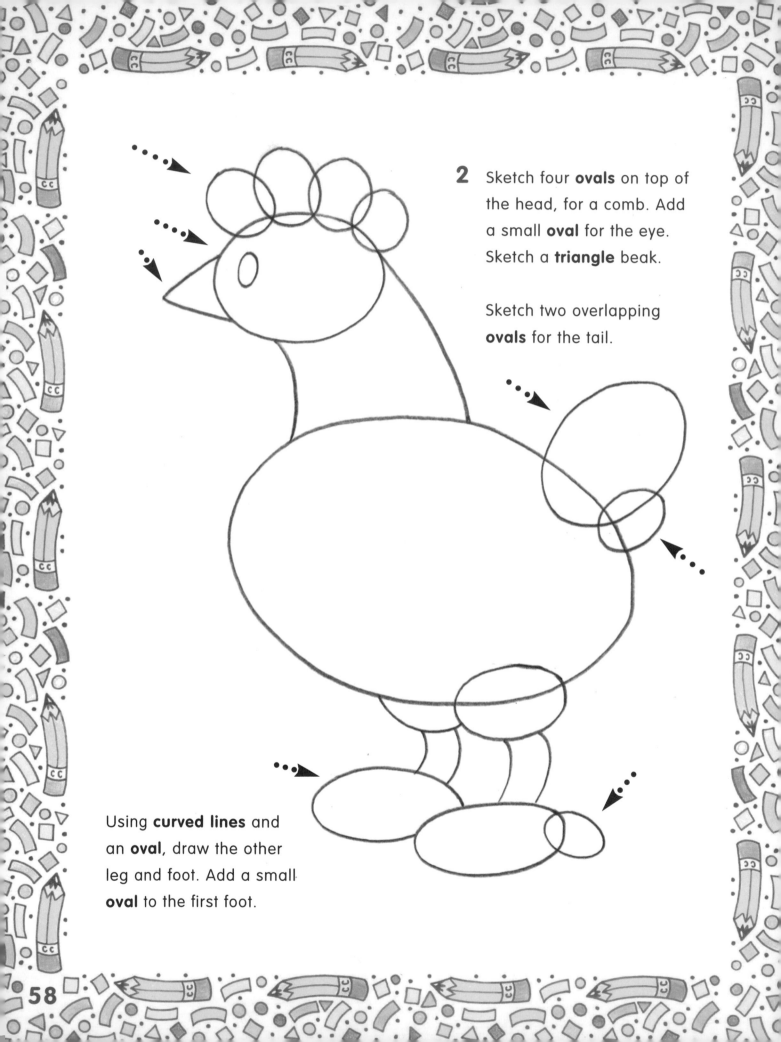

2 Sketch four **ovals** on top of the head, for a comb. Add a small **oval** for the eye. Sketch a **triangle** beak.

Sketch two overlapping **ovals** for the tail.

Using **curved lines** and an **oval**, draw the other leg and foot. Add a small **oval** to the first foot.

58

3 Darken part of the eye. Draw a **straight line** on the beak. Sketch two overlapping **ovals** for the rooster's wattle.

Sketch a large **oval** inside the body for the wing. Add two smaller **ovals** for the wing tips. Add **straight lines** to the feet.

4 LOOK at the final drawing! Erase the extra sketch lines. Darken the final lines. Color your rooster.

Wow! What a rooster! Congratulations! You are a GREAT artist!

Keep going!

Look at pictures of different animals. Look carefully at the basic shapes and lines that give them their unique look.

LOOK again, then sketch what you see.

Use the examples on this page and the next to practice, practice, practice . . .

. . . you will get better and your cartoons will get funnier!

You'll quickly see that you can draw many cartoon animals, starting with any shape you choose. You may even find that some of your cartoon animals begin to look like your friends, or teachers…

…but we'll save that subject for another time…!

Award yourself! On the next page you'll find an award certificate you can photocopy to let the world know you're a **Cartoonist's Apprentice First Class!**

Have you enjoyed this book?

Find out about other books in this series and see sample pages online at

www.123draw.com!

DATE _____

THIS IS TO CERTIFY THAT

HAS SUCCESSFULLY COMPLETED THE
"1-2-3 DRAW CARTOON ANIMALS" COURSE
AND IS NOW A

Cartoonist's
Apprentice
First Class

SIGNED _____
STEVE BARR